Günter Gerngross • Herbert Puchta

PLAYWAY 2

ACTIVITY BOOK

HELBLING

Unit 1

Hello again

1

❶ Listen and fill in the numbers (CD 1/1).

2

❷ Listen and draw (CD 1/2).

3 

4 

1

2

3

❸ Listen and fill in the numbers (CD 1/3). ❹ Listen and draw (CD 1/4). Find the pattern.

5

6

❺ Listen and circle (CD 1/5). ❻ Draw, colour and speak.

Unit 2

Vegetables

1 

1

______

2

______

3

______

4

______

5

______

1 Listen and write the names (CD 1/6). Speak.

2 

2 Look and speak. Write.

3 

4 

❸ Listen and fill in the numbers (CD 1/7). ❹ Think and draw.

5 

6 

❺ Listen and circle (CD 1/8). ❻ Colour and speak.

Unit 3

In the house

1 

1

2

3

4

1 Listen and tick (CD 1/9). Speak.

2

❷ Look and speak.

3

3 Listen and fill in the numbers (CD 1/10).

4 

1

2

3

4

4 Listen and speak (CD 1/11).

5

6

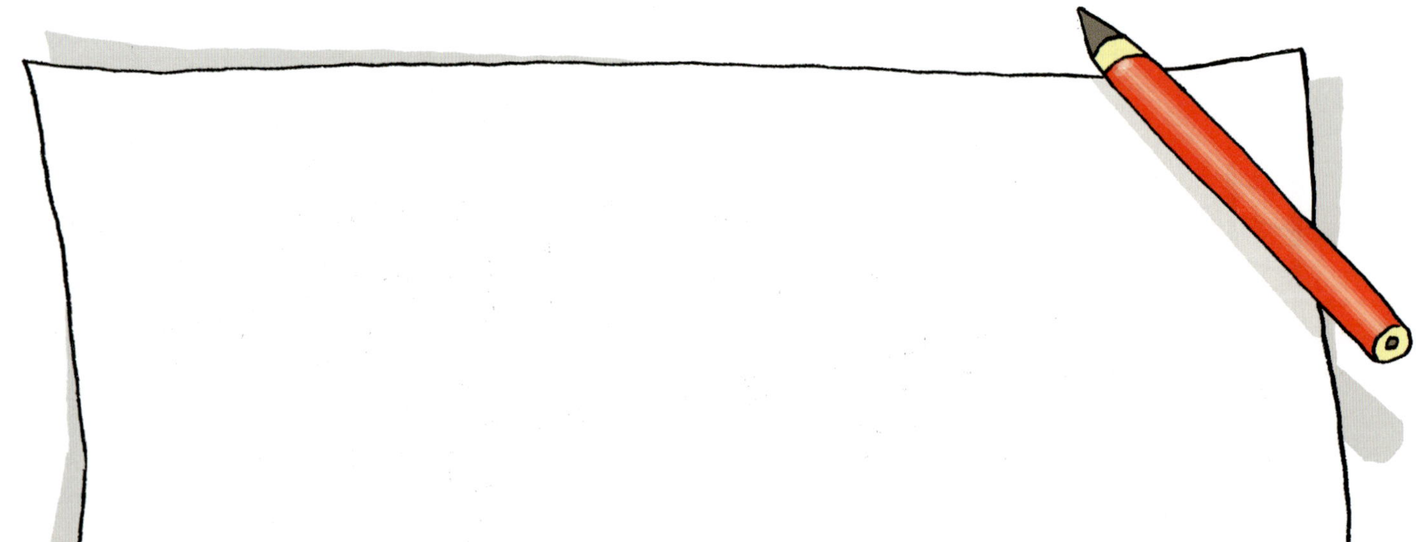

5 Listen and match (CD 1/12). 6 Draw, colour and speak.

Clothes

1

Frank   Debra   Mike   Susan

2

❶ Listen and match (CD 1/13). ❷ Listen and fill in the numbers (CD 1/14).

3

3 Listen and fill in the numbers (CD 1/15).

4

5

❹ Listen and colour (CD 1/16). ❺ Colour and speak.

Unit 5

Family

1 

1 Listen and fill in the numbers (CD 1/17).

2 

❷ Listen and fill in the numbers (CD 1/18).

3 

3 Look and follow the lines. Speak.

4

5

4 Listen and fill in the numbers (CD 1/19). 5 Find the odd one out.

Clever Joe

1 

100	90	80	70	60	50	40	30	20

❶ Listen and colour (CD 1/20).

2

② Listen and fill in the numbers (CD 1/21).

Clever Joe

3 

1  +  = £ 15

2  + 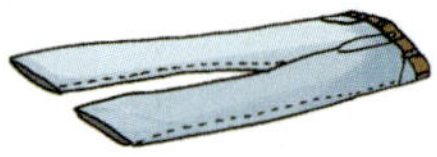 = £ ____

3 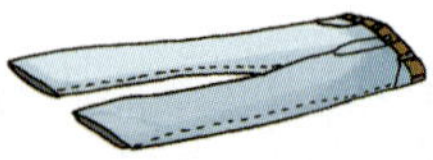 +  = £ ____

4  +  = £ ____

5  +  = £ ____

3 Look and do the sums.

4

5

4 Listen and draw lines (CD 1/22). 5 Look and colour the numbers. Speak.

Unit 7

Body

1

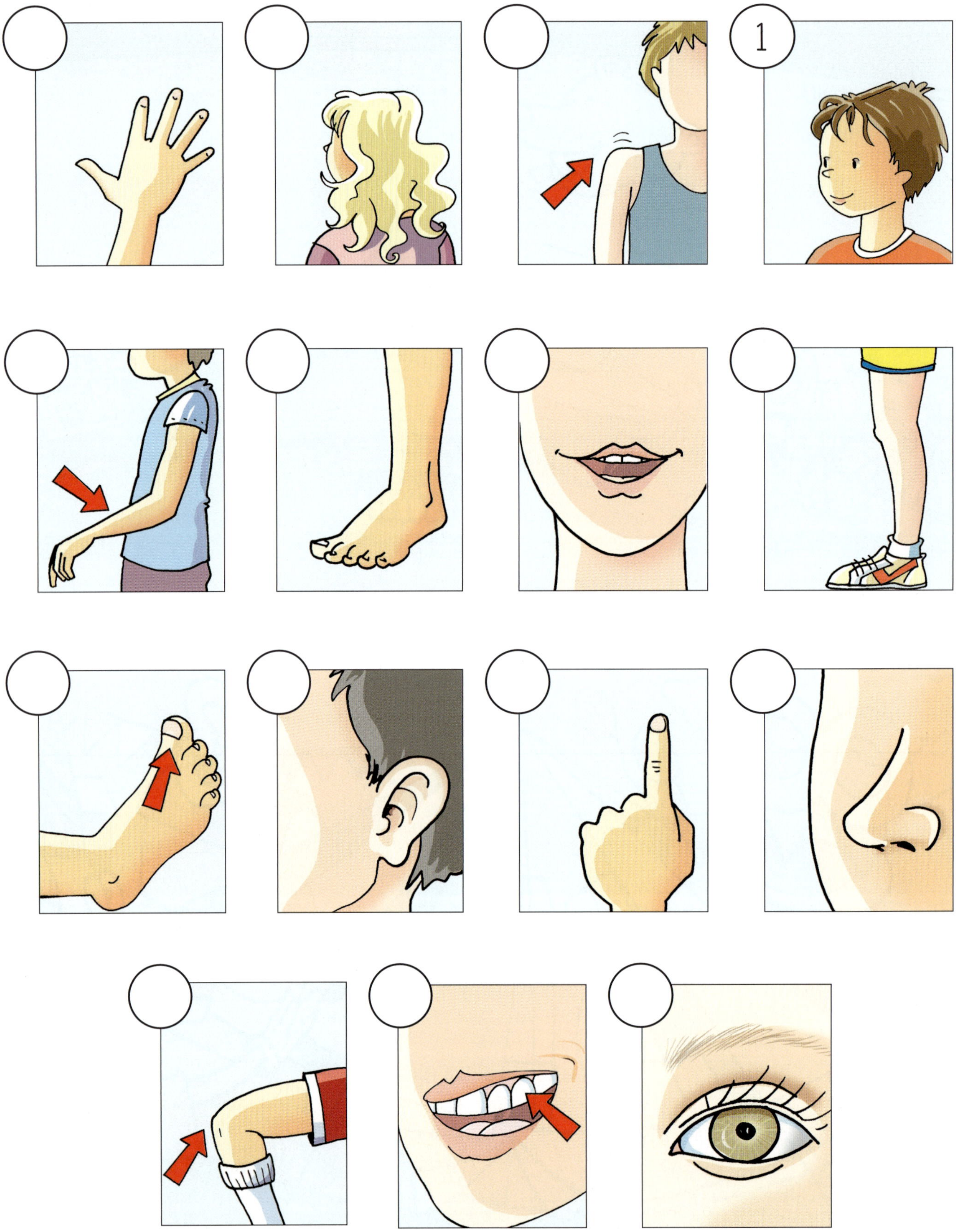

❶ Listen and fill in the numbers (CD 1/23).

2

❷ Listen and colour (CD 1/24).

3

4

3 Listen and fill in the numbers (CD 1/25). 4 Listen and circle (CD 1/26).

5

5 Listen and fill in the numbers (CD 1/27).

Unit 8

Farm

1  

1 Circle the animals. Colour them.

2 

3 

❷ Listen and fill in the numbers (CD 1/28). ❸ Draw and speak.

4

A

B

❹ Look and speak.

5

5 Listen and fill in the numbers (CD 1/29).

Travelling

1 

2 

❶ Listen and fill in the numbers (CD 1/30). ❷ Look and speak. Then draw and speak.

3 

Ella Tom ~~Polly~~ Patrick Mia Ken

____

____

____

Polly

____

____

3 Listen and write the names (CD 1/31).

4

4 Listen and fill in the numbers (CD 1/32).

5 

5 Listen and fill in the numbers (CD 1/33).

Unit

10 Holidays

1

A

B

2

1

❶ Look and speak. ❷ Listen and fill in the numbers (CD1/34).

3

❸ Listen and fill in the numbers (CD 1/35).

4

4 Listen and fill in the numbers (CD 1/36).